I0414878

Secrets to Popularity and Friendship

A Guide to Social Success

By
Meredith Trattler

ISBN: 0-7596-3015-1

This book is printed on acid free paper.

1stBooks – rev.05/22/02

Dedicated to my wonderful family and great friends

INTRODUCTION

A Look Ahead

By making the most of what you have, you can be a true social star. By developing your personality, demeanor, charisma, and talents, you can easily increase your popularity. You will be equipped with a repertoire of smooth social skills to attract new friends.

With your winning style, you will glow with inner social and self-confidence. At the same time you will feel personally rewarded. Your talent to benefit others will enhance your popularity. So you will be proud to be who you are.

With friends, you make great life gains. You share your excitement and good times. With their eye-awakening revelations, friends sometimes know you even better than you know yourself. Their compliments and support make you feel good about yourself.

At times you need answers to puzzling social questions and dilemmas. Many social situations are complex. With social savvy, you can make intelligent decisions to promote positive social outcomes.

Social success will help you to feel comfortable in your school environment. With your enthusiasm, you will excel in academic and extracurricular endeavors. Since you help others, you will feel gratified. Ultimately, you will maintain a healthy sense of well-being at school.

CHAPTER 1

For Sociability

1. Be friendly.

To be popular, socially interact with everyone. First, greet people enthusiastically. When you are in the halls at school, say hello and address classmates by name. With confidence, use eye contact, a smile, and an upbeat voice.

Everyone counts when it comes to saying hello. Strike up a conversation with acquaintances you do not usually talk to during lunch or in gym class. Peers describe popular students as friendly, social, outgoing, enthusiastic, helpful, cooperative, accepting, good-natured, good sports, supportive, and sympathetic.[1]

2. Get social exposure.

Be social with as many people as possible. This means be there. Be the partygoer, attending and throwing parties. Participate in extra-curricular activities, talk to acquaintances and friends after school, and visit other tables occasionally at lunch.

More people will get to know you well. If they have never met you previously, they will know who you are by your name and face. You will also project an image that you are outgoing and like to get involved.

You will make new friends. It is necessary for you to have contact, or share proximity, with those people with whom you would like to become your friends.[2] This gives them the chance to interact with you and get to know the real you. You may become friendly with people from class from being around them. You can join activities to make others. For example, joining the dance team, the cheer leading squad, the football team, or the baseball team may give you eventful social exposure to classmates you may want as friends.

3. Be receptive to others.

Wouldn't it be impressive if you could make everyone comfortable in your presence no matter how popular you are? Many people will like you for your easygoing manner. To help you be receptive, uncover valuable qualities that each individual has to offer. Focus on his or her good points. Ultimately, you will you will become friendly with those you may not have initially.

Show your interest in an acquaintance by making casual conversation and giving a compliment. Be inviting to those you may not have, or to those who do not expect it. Even if they do not accept this invitation, it will make them feel good that you wanted to include them.

With this attitude, you will gain friends. Sometimes you may want to think of popularity as a numbers game. Popular students have many friends. With your social skills, you will win over others one by one. It may seem that high school is filled with cliquish attitudes.[3] Yet you will be better liked for an attitude of mutual respect, tolerance, and approval of others for both their similarities and their differences. Moreover, you will make school a better place to be.

Compatible with being receptive, a feeling of equality characterizes the nature of friendship as teens. "Friendship is a dynamic, reciprocal relationship between two individuals."[4] In the teen years, friends feel equal to each other.[5]

4. Be enthusiastic.

If you can be enthusiastic, you shine like a bright star. Often smiling and laughing, your attitude is electric. You lift others to your level. Your upbeat manner gives your pals their daily dose of energy.

Your enthusiasm motivates you to action. You are the first to get involved. With smooth style, you round the extracurricular circuit of student organizations, school events, and sports teams. You want to do and then do more. Then you get the whole gang to come along for the wild ride.

5. Be outgoing.

When you talk to acquaintances, be an extrovert. At an appropriate time, you can talk to anyone who looks familiar or step up to introduce yourself to a new face. After you rap with the guy a few times, why not strike up some plans to play a few rounds of tennis? As you radiate with social confidence, you will expand your social horizons to make new pals.

For some people, being outgoing comes naturally. For others, being outgoing takes a little boldness. You do not have to send in a stunt double to do this trick. You can do it yourself. Become outgoing gradually if it does not come naturally to you. Talk to someone new once a day until you feel comfortable. The politeness of strangers or acquaintances may help you develop your skill. You will amaze yourself to discover how easy it becomes with practice. You will have newfound freedom to talk anyone in the "land of the free and the home of the brave."

6. Be agreeable, pleasant, and happy.

When you have a pleasant disposition, you will attract others. Act carefree, not often worried, distracted, or angry. If you worry and complain frequently, you will lose social points. Others will not be as happy in your company. So be upbeat, and go with the flow.

7. Be exciting.

A friend is great entertainment. A friend plays games and sports, jokes around, and shares favorite pastimes and interests. A friend is natural, comfortable, and easygoing when you do activities together. So let loose: grab your roller blades, pump up the CD volume, and swing your tennis racket. It is time for action. Your companionship is an important part of your friendship.[6]

To be sociable
➢ Be fired-up friendly.
➢ Be at a lot of activities.
➢ Be totally tolerant.
➢ Be extraordinarily enthusiastic.
➢ Be outstandingly outgoing.
➢ Be perfectly pleasant.
➢ Be extra exciting.

CHAPTER 2

To Solve Current Problems

How can students use social skills effectively to increase acceptance and diminish violence at school?

To be popular and make many friends, genuine behavior is essential. To enhance popularity, students learn it is in their best interests to be friendly to others of different races, religions, ages, abilities, and social crowds. They avoid aggression and violence since it makes them unpopular. Instead, they benefit others by helping, caring, and cooperating.

Can knowledge of social skills decrease negative peer pressure and promote academic success?

Students know that strong character and good personalities help make them popular. Yielding to negative peer pressure does not. They are aware their academic efforts facilitate social success.

Can popular behavior be learned?

Popularity is related to social skills, personality, inherent traits, and behavior. Researchers are able to measure popularity by the number of peers who select a classmate with whom to play, work, or be best friends.[1] Then researchers identify traits "correlated" or related to popularity.

These studies either confirm what seems obvious or illustrate new information. Yet, a problem exists with research that links traits to popularity. When two events happen together, this does not prove that one event is the cause and the other, effect. For example, being enthusiastic is correlated to peer popularity. However a person may be popular because he is enthusiastic or enthusiastic because he is popular. In a study performed on adolescents, one cannot assume similar results for children or adults without testing these groups too. Nevertheless, scientists frequently use correlational studies in psychology and medicine to draw conclusions about human behavior and health. In fact, some studies have shown that children can be coached to learn and practice certain behaviors to increase popularity with peers.[2]

How are popularity and friendship related?

Popularity and friendship are different. Yet both involve being liked. Popularity is determined by the degree your peer group likes an individual, while friendship refers to your liking a specific person.[3] Popularity and friendship can be examined at the same time since both are important experiences in your peer relationships.[4] You can utilize common social skills to enhance popularity and friendship.

CHAPTER 3

For Charisma

8. Be a pro at conversation to be able to talk to anyone.

Occasionally, it may be a stretch to have conversations with others. Maybe you go blank on what to say or become nervous. To gain attention from a classmate, show your interest. What interests pique him? What are her concerns? What are his activities? Can you give her a compliment?

A handy list of conversation starters includes current school, sports, and news events. Turn to the media with popular TV sitcoms, movies, and cultural trends. Rely on common values, hobbies, classes, and friends.

Conversation has a built-in advantage. As you talk about one subject, the subject will often remind you or link you to another idea. CLICK! With this cue, you can naturally say whatever comes to your mind next. This may rescue you from avoiding the dreaded LULL, a long silence in the conversation, which makes two people uncomfortable. Your acquaintance will appreciate your carrying the conversation. Talk as you would talk to a friend with whom you feel comfortable. If you talk easily to Kathy, talk to this person the same way. With practice, you will become assured and skilled.

When you converse, be courteous. If you are talking to one friend and a second person walks up, introduce the second person. Try to include this person by giving him or her chances to speak.

9. Positive remarks give positive results.

When you interact with others, be friendly and agreeable, not offensive or hurtful. Sure-fire ways to put others off are to to criticize, offend, be rude, yell at, or act condescending. If you embarrass, insult, or make fun of your classmates, you will make them feel ashamed. Acting bossy, too demanding, or disagreeable towards them rubs them the wrong way.[1]

Let's paint a better picture. More socially appropriate behavior is to talk to others in a pleasant, natural manner. Sometimes, you will sound straightforward and factual. Other times, be upbeat and comical. Give compliments for real achievements, or it is simply flattery.

Across age groups, scientific evidence supports that behaving in these positive ways is socially beneficial, while behaving in negative ways is detrimental. Unpopular teens demonstrate a tendency to say cruel comments to each other, along with starting fights.[2] Popular kids interact kindly. They make more positive verbal and nonverbal gestures to their peers.[3]

10. Show integrity and strong self-esteem by making good comments.

If you emphasize your friends' attractive qualities, other students will respect you and your friends. If you speak against your own friends, others may be wary you will do the same to them. Constantly making cutting remarks about your pals or casual acquaintances is a sign you are insecure about yourself.

11. Turn down an invitation politely.

Turn down an invitation, if you must, but agree on a future meeting at the same time. For example, "I would really like to go to the barbecue with you today, but I have plans with my family. Count me in next time." If you cannot make plans for a later date, do sound disappointed. If you avoid turning them down abruptly, a friend will feel better.

12. Communicate with confidence.

Speaking softly, not making eye contact with the person, or mumbling your words looks like you lack self-assurance. Speaking in a normal volume with eye contact and conviction causes others to listen. When you are explaining, be logical and complete, and leave out the *ums* and *likes*.

13. Be informed.

Glide along with today's techno trends. Be an avid user of technology to become a cyber star. The internet brings the whole world to you. Learning is limitless. To be informed locally and globally, glance at the newspaper every morning, and flip on the news at night. Being aware of current events in politics and business raises your stock, socially. Your awareness helps you fit in, and shows you are intelligent.

Partake in the hottest exercise trends. It is a good way for a chance encounter with your dream date at the gym, if you have not already met at your school or house of worship. While you exercise, why not listen to the tunes at the top of the charts? Then look to the professionals to read up on sports scores and stats. Follow the football and basketball draft picks and the prospective teams to win their division.

14. Be a leader.

Leaders are often popular. [4] Consider running for a club office such as president or treasurer, or head a sports team. While some students run for leadership positions routinely, it gives others the jitters. Yet there are ways to put you at ease for barrels of fun.

Leadership positions are available to you. Some take less effort to attain than others. First, select an activity where you can shine. It may be easier for you in the drama club than in a service organization. Second, determine an activity in which your pals participate. Since your friends would vote for you, you have a better chance of becoming an officer. Third, students will be more likely to elect you with experience. Your first year, start by heading a committee. Then run for a higher office. Being elected to a higher position can be a step-by-step process. A leadership position seems like hard work. However, the more effort you put into the group you choose, the more benefits you attain.

15. Show your talent.

Did you ever notice that a person became popular because he or she excelled at an activity? The quarterback of the football team, the star of the basketball team, and the President of the Student Council are usually popular. This is not the only way for you to be popular. However, it is a viable option if you find an activity easy enough to do.

Research supports the social benefits of becoming popular by standing out for an admirable accomplishment.[5] Upon interview, high school juniors assert students become popular when they gain recognition for good grades, belong to many organizations, or are successful in a sport.[6]

16. Develop your athletic talent.

Participate in at least one sport because it is an integral part of your social world. Athletics gives you expansive social opportunity. Act comfortably and be a good sport. You can play for some great laughs if you are not highly skilled. If you dislike competing, then swimming, biking, or aerobics are low contact sports without a score. If you feel outsized on or off the field, pump iron. Participation in sports is beneficial for friendship and social status. An outgoing athlete who is a sharp dresser may be a member of either the jock or the popular crowd.[7] While you do not have to be in the leading crowd to be popular, James Coleman surveyed thousands of high school students who reported that excelling in athletics was helpful for males, and having a good personality and reputation were important for all students to become part of the leading crowd.[8]

17. Invest time in your personality. Win with humor and creativity.

One way to have a good personality is to charm others with humor. Being witty can be a social plus.[9] Maybe you are the class clown or have a smooth delivery on a punch line. If not, all you need is some confidence and preparation. Have good jokes and witty one-liners for everyday situations.

At times, presentation makes comedy. Animate your facial expressions or make gestures. Use surprising sounds, tones, or volume. For example, let out a short shriek at the sound of good news.

Your friends will tell you classic one-liners. Play up their jokes by using them again in similar situations. This gives your buddies full credit, an ego boost, and double the laughs. From these, you will create a running stream of jokes between you and your friends.

As you converse with others, you will automatically think of your own lines impromptu. You can also create your own signature sayings, lingo, or nicknames. After you say a line, test your material. Watch to see if your friend laughs. If so, keep the joke in your repertoire.

Not only do you have to pay attention to what is humorous, but you also have to remember the humor. To remember a joke, tell it a few times shortly after you hear it. Give yourself permission to relax and let go. Do not worry about the blunders. The blunders can be comical too if you save yourself from the slip-up with another joke.

18. Invest time in your looks.

Your goal is to try to look your best, whatever that is for you. The first rule is to like what you have. Then look clean, neat, and well put together.

For females, become an expert at applying make-up. Use flattering colors, effective application, and appropriate amounts. The natural look goes a long way. Your best friend, magazines, and prime time television have hot beauty tips. From highlights to a great party getup, you can do a lot with your looks.

It would be comforting if looks did not matter and only what is inside counts. Your personality is very important for popularity, and a good personality may be all you need. Yet research shows that being attractive is linked to popularity. Still, you do not have to be very attractive to be popular.[10] Average looks may help you. Even with less, you can be popular. You see guys and girls at school who are popular but not good-looking. They receive recognition for other admirable characteristics. For instance, you probably know a popular person who wins over others because he or she is confident, outgoing, and witty.

19. Dress to impress.

Dress appropriately and match colors. Colors in nature look good together. Sets of tops, pants, or skirts look polished. Other students are live manikins. Check out what looks good on them. Take note of cool sensible-looking trends if you want to dress to fit in. Then select the attractive styles that flatter you.

Consider style, color, and fit for your fashion statement. To stand out in the crowd brights may do the trick. Occasionally you can dress a little offbeat to express individuality. However, do not alienate yourself with your attire. Wearing all black clothes continuously or wearing trench coats as in Columbine High School will make you an outcast.

Accessories such as shoes, shades, belts, jewelry, and handbags can dramatically enhance fashion flair. To be a sharp male dresser, sport some slick slacks, a sharp belt, and have your shirt smoothly tucked. High fashion hairstyles complement contemporary clothes. Dressing well can be expensive, so maintain a balance between the clothes you want and the clothes you can reasonably afford.

20. Put on your dancing shoes.

Time to sizzle at the next soirée. To dazzle your darling at the dance, practice before you are put on the spot. At home load Madonna, and crank the volume. Then sway those arms and swivel those hips. To polish your skills, consult a talented friend, MTV, or the gym's latest funk class to show you smooth sequences.

For Charisma
- ➤ Converse with finesse.
- ➤ Make positive remarks.
- ➤ Say good comments about friends.
- ➤ Turn down an invitation politely.
- ➤ Communicate with confidence.
- ➤ Be informed.
- ➤ Be a leader.
- ➤ Show your talent.
- ➤ Score with sports.
- ➤ Win with humor.
- ➤ Look your best.
- ➤ Dress to dazzle.
- ➤ Dance to the beat.

CHAPTER 4

For Successful Interaction

21. Make contact during your free time.

You can make friends from being in the same class. Yet class time may not be adequate to get to know others. In your free time, you interact with groups of friends outside of school. A group of about six friends forms a clique. In the late teen years, cliques associate together to form a crowd. Later, crowds diffuse into smaller groups of married couples. [1]

Increase your interaction to make more friends. Gym class is a good time during school for free interaction. Student government, sports teams, service organizations, and interest clubs are also helpful. In a study of high school students, those who participated in three or more extracurricular activities were more popular than those who participated in fewer.[2]

22. Mingle with those who you would like as friends.

If you are in high school, crowds of friends have particular behaviors or attitudes such as the jock crowd and the popular crowd. Some students can belong to more than one crowd.[3]   Other students feel crowds interfere with their sense of independence and individuality.[4] If you want to have friends in a certain crowd, join activities around school in which they participate.   By sharing interests, you develop friendships.[5]

Playing sports is an effective way to escape group boundaries. For many hours a day, you focus only on the sport. The issues of cliques and groups disappear.[6] So join football, volleyball, basketball or the cheerleading squad.

In your efforts to make friends, do not get discouraged. It may take time. If you find it hard to break through group boundaries, you may want to assert yourself with tact, when you have the opportunity. In a study of adolescent peer groups, those who became members of a clique had to push themselves into a group, and those who stood back were unsuccessful in being included.[7]

23. Be around people who want to be friends with you, who admire you, and who are supportive of you.

Some of your friends may seem buddy-buddy close, while others are there to hang out for fun. They are not there when the going gets tough. Your close relationships last a long time. Friends from high school could be your friends in adulthood or for life.[8]

High quality relationships give you a sense of emotional well-being. Close, supportive friendships enhance your self-esteem.[9] They make you feel worthy that others can appreciate your admirable qualities. They also give you a sense of security. In fact, children who have at least one close friend are protected from feelings of loneliness.[10]

Companionship, help, and emotional support make friendships last.[11] Attentive friends spend time with you. When you have a problem, supportive pals help. Reciprocate the benefits you receive from your friends to show your appreciation.

Be on the move
- ➢ It is never to late to circulate.
- ➢ Mingle with potential friends.
- ➢ Surround yourself with good friends.

CHAPTER 5

To Win Over Others

24. Focus on the individual with whom you are talking.

Make the person to whom you are talking feel #1. When you initiate a conversation, let your casual acquaintance talk about himself or herself. To express your interest, ask relevant, encouraging questions. Hot topics will be about the other person's world. So instead of focusing the conversation on you, focus it on another one in your crew. Then listen to a response.

Listening is major. People always like the guy or girl who listens. By listening, you will show that you are sincere. Genuine behavior like listening helps maintain strong friendships because you show that you care.

You will be a dashing diva or gregarious guy even when you are not telling amusing jokes, shooting one-liners, and keeping up with the latest trendy news. You will be impressive by showing regard for another's concerns. As an added benefit, you will never be at a loss for words. You will know what to say to a classmate. You can always talk about his or her interests. Research shows that unpopular children talked about themselves more when interacting with their mothers than popular children did.[1] If you focus on your friend's affairs, you will show him or her that you share a special common interest, your friend.

25. Show your kindness.

By fulfilling an act of kindness, you can easily gain a friend. It does not have to be an extravagant favor. Classmates will even appreciate small favors. Every day make it a goal to perform a simple, sincere act for another classmate.

If a hot girl/guy asks you to borrow paper, you might comment, "Okay. Just because you're cute." Or, as Mr. Moreinfo, review a theory a classmate did not catch in class. Do a 180 to put yourself in your classmate's shoes. Ask yourself, how would I like this theory explained to me if I did not understand? Then give it your best shot. After you have reached out to a classmate, this individual may reciprocate when you need a favor too. As a result, you are establishing a useful support network for times when you need it.

Prosocial behavior is behavior that "aids or benefits another person."[2] Examples of prosocial behavior are helping, cooperating, sharing, expressing sympathy, showing compassion, protecting, donating, and behaving altruistically.[3] Prosocial behaviors are related to being popular and having friends.[4] So these behaviors are your ticket to success.

26. Have a positive attitude.

A positive attitude is always refreshing for those in your company. Being upbeat can pull others up to your level. Your mood can be contagious. For a positive attitude, keep your dislikes about a situation or a person to yourself. The negative acts of complaining and criticisms are difficult for another person to hear. Your negative tone can bring others down.

How can you keep a positive attitude when an unfavorable event occurs? Some events are painful. Sometimes if a very difficult event occurs, you feel grief, pain, anger, and sadness. Your parents and friends may help you to feel better if you discuss the situation with them. If you feel overwhelmed, seek profession help.

In time, after you have grieved, you will start to feel better and heal. You may be able to adopt a more positive outlook then. Your attitude will help you to feel better. You might figure out a viable way to solve your problem. Or you could identify some good things that happened in an unfixable situation.

In the same way, you can talk back to yourself when you have an unpleasant thought. For example, if you do not do well on a test, do not lose hope. Instead, tell yourself you did not leave enough time to study. Next time you will study harder without a marathon cram session. If you did not understand a theory, you will go to the teacher for a brush-up session. Then an

"A" will be on the way. Positive thoughts can help you in relationships, jobs, and goals. For every negative, there is a rewarding positive to improve your outlook. An unfortunate event may even be an opportunity in disguise.

27. Have good intentions.

If you have good intentions for others, you'll be playing fair ball. However, your friends and acquaintances will notice if you manipulate, act selfishly, and behave dishonestly. If you act disloyal to friends, you will foul the other players. Before you know it, you could be out of the game.

If you want to keep a good friend, be loyal. This will strengthen your friendships. By the teen years, loyalty, trust, and genuineness are an important part of friendships, and disloyalty and lack of trust are common reasons for terminating friendships.[5]

28. Share.

From kindergarten, you learned values that win over your classmates. Along with having good intentions for classmates, share to show you care. Lending the must-haves, from school supplies to the perfect third date outfit, will earn big points. For a birthday or a just-because memento, gifts strengthen relationships. Friends appreciate sharing and generosity.[6]

You share activities with a friend.[7] As teens, you talk about your ideas, opinions, and experiences. You often reveal inner thoughts and feelings, which can make friendships stronger.[8] If you share personal information, you may want to be sure that it is appropriate and you trust whom you tell.

29. Be perceptive by paying attention to how others feel. Practice compassion.

Do you remember a situation when you were speaking to a friend, then noticed by his facial expression and tone of voice that he was upset? Then you responded appropriately by asking what was wrong so that you could help. Be understanding when a friend's life does not go his or her way. After listening to a friend tell a problem, say, "I am upset that this has happened. I feel bad for you. You must really be upset." Just by saying these simple words, you console your friend. Send a message: If this happened to me, I would feel the same way you do.

Your friend will probably feel much better. He might tell you how he is going to solve his problem. However, if the problem still confuses him, do not feel pressured to offer a solution. You have already helped a great deal since you have shown him that you understand how he feels. Well-liked classmates are often perceptive and empathetic to their peers' feelings, so reading your classmates emotions well and responding appropriately may help you interact with others successfully.[9]

30. Be encouraging.

Another great way to win over someone is to encourage the person to realize his or her full potential. If you believe in a friend's ability, this can be one of the greatest gifts you give. If you see that someone is a talented artist like Picasso or a great vocalist like Barbra Streisand, let him or her know. You affirm that your friend stands out from the crowd. You could also be the catalyst for him or her to pursue a new goal.

31. Give compliments.

A simple way to win over a classmate is to give him or her a classy compliment. When you tell Brian that he is a real riot and Cindy that she is a true brain, they have instant boosts to their egos. Let a person know he or she is the deluxe cheeseburger with a side of fries and an extra large shake.

32. Do not act like a snob.

Acting superior to others will cause resentment towards you. With an I-am-better-than-you-attitude, you will gain few fans and friends. Each person likes to feel important.

One way to earn friends is to put an acquaintance on a pedestal with your praise. You can also earn a friend by being a warm person who makes an acquaintance feel comfortable in your presence. Because of your receptive manner, more classmates will like you. Being the Ice King/Queen will not get you where you want to go. Scientific evidence shows that unpopular peers were characterized as stuck up.[10] So lose that attitude.

To win over others
➤ Focus on his or her world.
➤ Be kind.
➤ Radiate a positive attitude.
➤ Play the good intentions game.
➤ Share to show you care.
➤ Be perceptive and compassionate.
➤ Give the gift of encouragement.
➤ Give classy compliments.
➤ Lose an attitude.

CHAPTER 6

For Academic and Social Success

33. Give it your best shot academically.

Your academic goal is to learn. Doing well in your schoolwork also helps your social success and confidence. Maybe you are the talented one to set the curve. If not, do not feel intimidated because other students are smarter. Do your work as well as you can. If you want to improve, there are loads of techniques. Ask the teacher for extra help after school, or get a trusty tutor.

Make file cards of facts or formulas that you have to memorize before the test. During free time, you can flash a few file cards to review test material. Reread the chapters on the test. Give yourself extra time to study for a difficult test. After you learn the material, study with a friend and quiz each other. By being conscientious, you can improve your grades.

Your academic effort is socially beneficial. Scholastic success and cognitive abilities are positively associated with popularity.[1] Males with the image of an athlete scholar are more popular than those with the image of an athlete.[2] The social benefits of academic success are apparent when hardworking students land great jobs later in life. Oprah Winfrey was voted most popular in high school.[3]

34. Learn lectures effectively.

Taking notes well provides a good foundation for study. Prior to the class lecture, read the assigned chapters. You will understand difficult concepts, and you will take better notes. Even if you fall behind in the reading, read the current text that the teacher will discuss, then backtrack later.

35. Write with eloquence.

It is not only what you say, but how you say it. Check grammar, punctuation, and spelling. Use active voice and proper verb tense. Replace repetitive words with synonyms. When your paper flows smoothly, your teacher understands the points you are making.

Your presentation is important. Type your papers and place them in folders with cover pages. Artful spacing and headings also helps.

36. Flash your brights.

Some ways you appear to be smart are to have common sense, use good judgment, have a sense of humor, be creative, have wisdom, be perceptive, and have a good memory. Hitting it off with a group demonstrates you are sharp interacting with people. Using leadership ability to help others shows intelligence.

37. Get on your teacher's good side.

The first student to bring an apple to the Teach had the right idea. If the teacher likes you, you will get more positive exposure in the classroom.[4]   Arrive on time, be organized, pay attention, and participate in the class discussion. Be respectful, kind, and friendly. Students observe the teacher's attitude towards you. If the leader of the class likes you, this attitude could set a tone for your other classmates to treat you the same way.

38. Be competent in managing your work.

In folders, organize your class notes and homework. To prevent searching for items, designate permanent places for important papers. Make a list of your daily responsibilities. Then group them according to priority. As you complete each, cross it off the list. Keep a calendar for your work. If you are overloaded, write down a plan. Dedicate the appropriate amount of time to each subject.

Electronic organizers are like having a mini brain. You can mark notes on a schedule, set an alarm, use a calculator, and access all of your friends' phone numbers and birthdays at a touch of a button. An organizer is a quick, easy-to-use asset for organization.

39. Pay attention.

A class follows a plan. When the teacher speaks, students listen. When the teacher gives an assignment, students are conscientious. Instead you may be drifting off to this weekend's rockin' bash.

Fight the inclination to feel maxed out. Move along with the class plan. Popular students spend less time daydreaming. They spend more time paying attention and working on tasks than unpopular students.[5] If the students are working efficiently to complete a project, attune yourself to the group. You can use these smarts outside of class too. Are the students fired up for the rival high school football game? Let loose and pump up the volume with the others.

40. Be mindful of your image.

At school you want to show others that you have your act together, not just with your work, but as a person. To look well kept, keep your mane tame. Your hair should have been recently cut and styled, and your body, clean. Before your daily routine, jump into the shower and lather up with the latest aromatherapy body wash in lavender and chamomile. A quick splash of perfume or cologne makes good sense. Be stocked with mints to be safe.

Dive into bed so that you can bounce out with at least eight hours of sleep. Not only will you look better, but you will also have energy, be in a good mood, and feel positive. A loaded class lecture will be easier to handle awake.

When you arrive at school, be calm. Even when you are not part of the freshman welcoming committee, be easygoing and attentive to others. If you arrive complaining, in a panic about your dilemma of the week, or cramming for a European history exam, you will look frazzled.

41. Manage stress effectively.

Because certain situations can make you anxious, you wear your emotions on your sleeve occasionally. This is normal and acceptable.

It is not an attractive to act stressed in front of students frequently. When you are stressed, you are frustrated, irritable, and complain. This alienates others.[6] Anxious children tend to be less popular than those children who are not anxious.[7] It is advantageous to be happy and relaxed in social settings.

To solve a problem, you can talk to friends and family if you are unable to find a worthy solution yourself. When you have time to talk in private, you can solve a problem well. If you cannot wait until after school, pull your pal backstage. You do not want an audience for your production.

How do you cope with stress that occurs in daily life? Exercise at least three times a week. Exercise is beneficial for your mind and body. Exercise elevates your mood to make you happier. It gives you a sense of well-being, and strengthens your confidence. Your body benefits from aerobic activities such as walking, jogging, and biking. You can lift weights for muscle strength and definition. Yoga promotes physical flexibility and mental relaxation. Select a sport that you enjoy to keep you motivated. With a friend, you will have someone to keep you company and on track.

Other activities can also help reduce stress. Go for a walk outdoors. The sun and nature sounds have a calming effect. Step away from your daily routine by reading a favorite book or spending time with family and friends. For twenty minutes a day, lie on your bed, listen to calming music or relaxation tapes. Breathe in through your nose and out through your mouth slowly. Clear your mind, and relax all of your muscles for a peaceful break.

42. Be goal-oriented.

Make achievement an important value. To keep on track, select an interest that really drives you. What puts locomotion into your motion? Find a meaningful purpose such as helping others or pursuing your dream.

After you decide, make a plan. How are you going to accomplish this goal? Realistically, how long will it take? By surrounding yourself with motivated friends, you will be motivated too. As you attain goals, admiration from peers can improve your popularity.[8]

To make the grade for glitz
- Hit the books.
- Learn lectures effectively.
- Write well.
- Shine with sense.
- Get on your teacher's good side.
- Be organized.
- Pay attention.
- Maintain a good image.
- Manage stress successfully.
- Go for goals.

Chapter 7

For Emotional Development and Growth

43. Be your #1 fan.

Learn to feel good about yourself. If you doubt yourself sometimes, do not feel discouraged. Everyone gets a little shaky with self-doubts at times.

There are some simple, magical tricks to help you feel good about yourself. Set your mind to your mantra: "I believe in me." Build a handy list of your strengths. Listen to your friends since they tell you why you are a big shot to them. Then, find what you are good at and do it. Finally, organize your goals. You will feel first-rate when you have a plan. When you are in doubt, glance over your list of strengths, talents, and goals to give yourself positive reinforcement.

Your outlook can significantly affect the way you view yourself so be POSITIVE. Not only will you shine in your classmates' eyes, but your self-image will also skyrocket. If you tell yourself, "I will never be able to make the tennis team," answer that you are qualified because you practice regularly.

44. Take care of yourself. Eat right, exercise regularly, and rest adequately.

Three times a day, eat healthy, full meals, and snack on wholesome foods for energy. To reduce stress, stay fit, and maintain a sense of well-being, exercise regularly. Then rest sufficiently to recharge for your active lifestyle.

45. Help others.

Select your favorite charity to join. By redirecting your focus from yourself to others, you will feel better about yourself. When you help others, you forget about your own problems. You establish a valuable sense of worth and purpose by taking a hands-on approach to help solve the world's problems. Celebrities and mega companies promote charities all of the time. It's time for you to do honorable, kind acts too. You'll be someone's hero in a snap.

46. Try not to be shy or self-conscious. It is self-defeating.

If you are shy, your classmates will not get to know the real you. Your kindness, helpfulness, and interest in them will not be apparent. Acting shy may prevent you from being social. Studies show that being shy and withdrawn is not socially advantageous.[1] Luckily, you know ways to make friends and be well-liked.

Instead of acting shy, debut the real you. Take a risk because being shy may be even riskier.

Around others you will try to be enthusiastic, sincere, and pleasant. Who would not want a friend like this? Besides, you know what to say to all the kids on the block. Just talk to them about their interests and listen.

Practice using compliments or witty lines with good friends. See their positive reactions. Tell yourself that you can do the same with the people you want to know better. For those moments when you are too jittery to be confident, pretend you are the social star whom you admire in English class. Say what you think he or she would say in the same social situation. Then—poof—your shyness could disappear.

To feel groovy
➢ Be your #1 fan.
➢ Take care of your body.
➢ Choose your charities.
➢ Shy away from shyness.

CHAPTER 8

For Your Reputation and Character

47. Be honest and trustworthy. Keep your word.

A person learns quickly whether he can trust you. Trust is a very important part of friendship. If a person confides in you, sshhh. Keep secrets. Keeping information confidential is an important part of being a perfect pal. Your friends may more easily disclose information about themselves to you as their confidante, and this will strengthen your friendships.[1] They will tell you their latest crush, or they will ask your opinion on a personal matter. You can be the up-in-coming Ann Landers of your group. Ultimately trust and honesty promote strong, healthy friendships.

When two pals end a friendship, the cause is often a lack of trust.[2] To keep your friendships on track, ask yourself some questions. Am I considerate of my friend's well-being? Am I honest? Am I there when he or she needs one? Am I loyal? You may like hanging out with some friends for a good time. These friends may not be there for you when you have a problem. By being dependable, you achieve close, lasting friendships.

48. Show integrity.

Another valuable trait that people admire is integrity -- acting ethically by doing the right thing. Key examples of integrity are being honest, fair, and dependable. When you have to make a decision, use your reason, intuition, and experience to decide the right choice. When you face obstacles or conflict with others, before you act, consider the consequences. Also consider alternative modes of action. Is there a better way? If you are stumped, do not be impulsive. Take time to figure it out. Some situations are complex. Ultimately, ethical principles serve as a guide in making decisions.

49. Be dependable.

Let others know that there are no rainouts with you. Come rain or shine you are there. If others know that they can count on you to partake in activities, they will invite you. "Sign me up!" might be your new slogan.

Be there for curtain call. Being on time means you need to plan ahead. If you are usually fifteen minutes late, get ready as if your meeting were fifteen minutes earlier.

Along with social gatherings, be a dependable participant in extracurricular activities. Ready for action? Be the first to volunteer for leadership roles, such as chairing committees. Responsibly complete all of the work for the organization's projects. To be an effective leader, focus on accomplishing group goals. The group members will really appreciate your contribution, leadership, and dependability.

50. Be respectful of others.

Use manners in the lunchroom. Work quietly in the library. Thank the server at restaurants. Not only will you be considerate, you will also be polished.

When you go to break bread with the group, try to be patient. Realize that when others are serving you, it is often a group effort. The restaurant kitchen may be running slowly instead of, like you, on the go. Yet one person does not have control over every step in the process. So why yell at the waiter when the food does not come on time? Remember that those who provide services to you have difficult, physically demanding jobs.

Respect your mother, father, educators, and friends. They help you and give you a sense of well-being. Your regard will promote good relationships with them.

51. Be happy for someone else's good fortune.

Suppose a friend wins the lead in the class play, or an acquaintance joins the tennis team. Do not envy others for their success. Be thankful for their accomplishments. They are role models that show you success is possible. If it can happen for them, it can happen for you. Friends sense your sincerity. If you are happy for them, they will see your support. Jealousy is also an unproductive emotion.

For a cool rep
- ➢ Be honest.
- ➢ Have integrity.
- ➢ Be dependable.
- ➢ Be respectful.
- ➢ Do not envy.

CHAPTER 9

To Be Well-Liked in a Group

52. Learn to join the group skillfully.

You may be invited, or you may initiate contact with a group. How do you cut into dance? Enter at an appropriate time. According to Asher, Renshaw, and Hymel, popular children may wait for an interruption in an activity to join in.[1] During a break in the game or conversation, slide in.

Unpopular kids often act aggressively and are disruptive.[2] This may be reflected in their style for entering a group activity. According to research by Dodge, Schlundt, Schockenand, and Deluggach (1983) and Putallaz (1991), unpopular children often disrupted the group activity, made comments about themselves, and disagreed with other peers. Yet popular children maintained a frame of reference to the group's activity, making relevant comments to the task at hand.[3] So focus on the group, not yourself.

On the field, get in the huddle to hear the play. When it's time to battle it out with the competition, give acknowledgement to an opponent and hide your frustration. If you are playing tennis, and you miss a difficult shot, do not show your disappointment by tossing your racket. Instead, compliment your opponent on hitting an amazing shot. Play by the rules, and include others so they have a chance to play. At the end of the game, shake hands. You will look good no matter what the score is at the end of the game.

53. Avoid trouble, starting fights, and bullying others.

Maybe someone angered you, upset you, or did not give you your way. Avoid starting fights, violence, bullying, insulting, and excluding. Aggressive behaviors are related to being unpopular in school.[4]

These behaviors hurt your reputation. Your reputation influences your popularity. High school adolescents have recognized the importance of having a good reputation and personality to be popular in school.[5] Teens who are cruel and bossy, pick on others, and cause trouble are unpopular.[6]

54. Know what to do when conflict occurs.

Friendship is easy when everyone is happy-go-lucky and getting along. Yet disagreement occurs. If a situation bothers you, tell your friend. At an appropriate time, say, "I was upset when this situation occurred." Talk calmly. Do not place blame. Then, he or she will be less likely to get defensive. It is more likely that the conflict will be resolved.

If you are having difficulty resolving a disagreement, try to compromise. Conflict arises between friends from issues of trust. Resolve conflict by talking things out and negotiating.[7] As you meet halfway and each receives requests, you feel equally important. Effective problem solving will help protect your friendships.

If you can forgive and be friends again, great. If a friend has hurt you too badly, and you call it quits, still be cordial. To hold a grudge is to make an enemy. Your crowd may be uncomfortable when you two do not get along, and you do not want to be left out of a social outing involving him or her.

55. Do not compromise your morals.

Even if a friend tries to influence you to go against your conscience, do not listen. A true friend will not put you in a bad situation. Just as a supportive companion can have a positive influence on you, one who acts negatively may have a bad influence on your behavior.[8] He may influence you to do poorly in school or act negatively. If you argue with friends, you may be inclined to do the same with teachers or other adults.[9] Or they may try to influence you to do illegal activities.[10] Jail will be your new hangout. Drugs and cigarettes ruin your health, sense of well-being, self-worth, family life, and schoolwork. You become addicted to these chemical substances before you even realize it, and then it is too late. Think smoking cigarettes is not so bad? Who wants to kiss a smoker?   Cigarettes   cause   serious   health consequences, bad breath, and wrinkles around lips.

Drugs do not make you popular in school. Sexual activity does not determine your popularity. Both of these activities can ruin your image. A good personality and good character are most important for popularity. Your goal is to make friends who have a good influence on you, uphold strong values, and have a positive effect on your well-being.

For group interaction
- ➤ Slide in the group skillfully.
- ➤ Avoid starting fights, causing trouble, and damaging your reputation.
- ➤ Handle conflict with compromise.
- ➤ Stay away from immorality and illegality.

CHAPTER 10

To Get Along Well with Others

56. Help.

You will stand out from the crowd if you volunteer. Look for ways to help. When you are asked to do a favor, be glad because you will score points socially. Be the first to help, and you will be noticed.

Helpfulness and generosity are important features of friendships.[1] By helping an acquaintance, you may make a new friend. By giving help to close friends, your friendships may grow even stronger.

57. Cooperate.

Be a team player. When you work on a team project, you may be able to form friendships. As you work together, you organize, problem solve, and share. With your assistance and your enthusiasm, the group will be proud to have you on their team. You will be fourth at bat, clean-up hitter.

Cooperation also involves good negotiation skills.[2] To be a good sport, you have to compromise when you do not get your way. Changes often occur so that everyone can work together successfully. You have to tolerate unwanted hassles when the group goes into overtime to complete a project, or the meeting is rained out and rescheduled.

Be a switch hitter. Do not focus only on your best bud. Pay attention to and converse with each player. Every team member deserves a chance to contribute and likes acknowledgement.

If you are captain of the team, be reasonable in assigning the work. To avoid seeming bossy, ask others politely to participate. Explain reasons for assigning certain tasks and deadlines. As a leader, use good organization skills and a good plan.

Remember to be personable. Cut the grating criticism, starting fights over work, or being condescending to others. Instead, be ready to compliment. Play up the rookie's bright idea and the shortstop's efficiency. With encouragement, your peers will work harder because you have recognized their efforts. In the final inning, you will win the game if you have contributed to the group's success and gotten along well with its members.

58. Do not be self-absorbed.

How can you avoid the trap of being self-involved? Instead of your own interests, be inclined to focus on other classmates' concerns. How do you do this? In all capitals... REACH OUT. Be sociable, perform kind gestures, listen, be perceptive of others' needs, give compliments, be dependable, and help. If you are merely concerned with yourself, your activities, and your problems, you will not pay adequate attention to others, and you will lack an appealing style to make many friends and be popular.

59. Use self-control.

You want to use self-control so that you can be considerate to others. If you use self-control, you often recognize other people's needs and feelings, not simply your own. You do the right things and avoid those that you should not do just because you may feel like it at the spur of the moment. Using self-control can be an important element for your smooth social style.

To be self-controlled, avoid starting fights. Let's say Joe Shmoe made you angry. Do not physically hurt him or damage his belongings. It is that simple. If you do, your own rep will take a hit. And you will hurt your image. Others will look at you unfavorably, and you'll risk losing friends. Research shows that unpopular kids often act in aggressive ways.[3]

To attain certain goals, you need self-control. At times, you may have to skip social events so that you have adequate time to study to receive good grades. Your efforts will pay off when you are accepted to college. This is one type of self-control, *delay of gratification*. Delay of gratification means that you put off immediate rewards to receive even greater rewards later. Some factors that affect one's ability to delay gratification are age, length of time to wait, the belief that the reward will finally be received, and prior success or failure.[4] If you were to become a doctor, you must attend college, medical school, internship and residency. This takes time away from social activities and requires hard work. Later on, you would attain a gratifying, prestigious career. So strong self-control can contribute to your success. Good things come to those who wait.

60. Be mature.

Using self-control shows maturity. On the other hand, being obnoxious can be an immature way to put others off.[5] Acting like a loud, weepy third-grader when you are in tenth will give the gang some nightmarish flashbacks.

Being mature can be reflected in your demeanor and mind. Carry yourself with confidence and dress appropriately for your age. Keep up with attitudes, ideas, knowledge, and wisdom appropriate for your age. Helping others and being dependable shows maturity. Adults may be excellent role models for maturity. You may want a parent or another adult as a friend. Some teens feel that their mother is a best friend to them.[6] Parents or adults can give you a mature perspective, one you can not figure out alone. Parents have been through what you are going through so they may have some hearty advice.[7] Their ideas can be instrumental for decision making.[8]

To hit it off with the team

➢ Lend a helping hand.
➢ Be cooperative.
➢ Reach out.
➢ Use self-control.
➢ Be mature.

CHAPTER 11

To Make Many Friends

61. Prepare with skills.

When you see a student you do not know be the confident, friendly one. Smile, say hello, and introduce yourself. He or she may be the hot kid that you high-five in the halls someday. Take the initiative to introduce a new kid on the block to others.

Remember to be the social star who is friendly and talks to all. If you want to talk to an acquaintance, but are at a loss for words, pique his or her insatiable desire for the genuine compliment. After you initiate a conversation, let your new friend do the talking. You do the listening. Look at your friend, and pay attention. Do not go off on an ego trip of your own.

Chit chat about a common class or interest. Be happy, enthusiastic and positive. Plan a common ground activity. "Golf this Saturday?"

Be inviting to acquaintances you have made through friends. You are familiar to them and have received good recommendations. Show you are excited to see them. Greet them with a big smile and enthusiasm to make them feel first-rate.

If you want someone to know you admire him or her, tell a close friend who will relay the compliment. When you see the person later, you will be more likely to hit it off.

Popular students usually have many friends. Skills to make friends could help your popularity. In a study by Oden and Asher, a group of fourth graders, who had difficulty making friends, became more popular after they were given coaching to participate in a group, cooperate by taking-turns, communicate by talking and listening, and support others with help and attention.[1] By learning and practicing certain behaviors, it is possible to become more popular.

62. Make mental notes.

A sharp way to start a conversation is to remember information Rachel told you in a previous conversation. If she mentioned she was going skiing, ask her about her trip when she returns. Show that you are interested in what's happening in her world.

63. Invest time.

Spend quality time palling around. With seven days in a week and twenty-four hours in a day, you are teeming with time. If you are too busy, it could strain your friendships. Do your best to juggle school priorities and social activities.

64. Watch how others make friends.

To help you accomplish a goal, find a role model. Hang out with the girl or guy in gym class who is loaded with friends, and pick up how-to tips. Mr. or Miss Popularity can give you hints. You may be able to do a routine activity together. Study for a test or drive to school together if you cannot spend time together socially. In turn, utilize your repertoire of social skills. Soon, you will be on the invite list to join him or her.

65. Learn from your siblings.

Other kids and teachers may know you as Jeff's younger brother or sister. If your sibling is older, he could offer you mature insight. Maybe your sib's a true social talent, popular with lots of pals. Use him as a role model. He or she can give you trusty advice on how to act for certain social situations and dilemmas. What does your sib do that boosts his or her social life? What are the top-rated activities? Even if you have conflicts with your sib now and then, your sibling may offer significant social learning experiences.[2]

To make many pals
- ➤ Be set with skill.
- ➤ Make mental notes.
- ➤ Invest time.
- ➤ Get a gifted guru.
- ➤ Learn savvy from your sib.

CHAPTER 12

To Make the Most of the *Secrets*

66. Be comfortable and enjoy yourself.

Be cognizant of these guidelines, and be ready to use them spontaneously. When you socialize, act naturally. You do your best when you are relaxed. If you get nervous, you will get discouraged and will probably not socialize well. People who do the best socially are the people who are glad when others like them. However, they do not get too affected if someone does not.[1] Besides, if someone does not like you, just remember, they do not have good taste!

Along with acting naturally and comfortably, you want to keep your true character. While following these guidelines, do not feel as if you are trying to mold yourself into a different person. Since these social skills bring out the best in you, you will keep your true character while you utilize them. This is the way you will be able to excel socially, be self-confident, and be yourself.

67. Be goal oriented and consistent.

By mastering a few points at a time, you can be efficient. You may want to combine a complex social skill with one that is a snap. Give yourself time to be proficient in guidelines that require added effort. By creating a schedule and checking off achieved guidelines, you can be successful.

68. Be socially astute.

Becoming popular requires a person to act geniunely towards others. Some people may not be as receptive, helpful, and dependable as you are. Be glad you realize the social merit of you considerate style. Your genuine character makes you attractive to others so you enhance your popularity. Your efforts bring out the best in you, and social success is your reward.

In action
➢ Be natural.
➢ Be consistent.
➢ Be genuine.

Meredith Trattler

NOTES

Chapter 1

1. N. E. Gronlund and L. Anderson, Personality characteristics of socially accepted, socially neglected and socially rejected junior high school pupils. *Educational Administration and Supervision* 43 (1957): 329-338; W. W. Hartup, Peer interaction and social organization, in P.H. Mussen, ed., *Carmichael's Manual of Child Psychology* Vol. 2, 3rd edition (New York: Wiley, 1970) pp. 388-389; K. W. Gentry and N. Miller. Sociometric indices of children's peer interaction in the school setting, in H. C. Foot, A. J. Chapman, J. R. Smith, eds., *Friendship and Social Relations in Children* (New York: Wiley and Sons, 1980), p. 151; Hartup, W. W. Peer relations, in P. H. Mussen, Series Ed., *Handbook of Child Psychology* Vol. 4, 4th edition (New York: Wiley, 1983), p. 133.; Newcomb, Bukowski, and Pattee, Children's peer relations: a meta-analytic review of popular, rejected, neglected, controversial, and average sociometric status, *Psychological Bulletin* 113 *(1993)* 99- 128; D. Elkins, Some factors related to the choice status of ninety eighth-grade children in a school society, *Genetic Psychology Monographs*, 58 (1958): 223; W. Loban, A study of social

sensitivity (sympathy) among adolescents. *Journal of Educational Psychology* 44 (1953): 102-112; and J. D. Coie, K. A. Dodge, and H. Coppotelli, Dimensions and types of social status: a cross-age perspective, *Developmental Psychology 18* (1982): 557-570.

2. J. Epstein, The selection of friends: changes across the grades and in different school environments, in T. Berndt and G. Ladd, eds., *Peer Relationships in Child Development* (New York, Wiley: 1989), p. 159; and J. Epstein, Friendship selection: developmental and environmental influences, in E. C. Mueller and C. R. Cooper, eds., *Process and Outcome in Peer Relationships* (San Diego: Academic Press, 1986), p. 154.

3. B. Brown, The role of peer groups in adolescents' adjustment to secondary school, in T.J. Berndt and G.W. Ladd, eds., *Peer Relationships in Child Development* (New York: Wiley and Sons, 1989), p. 188.

4. D. I. Burk, Understanding friendship and social interaction, *Childhood Education* 72 (1996): 282-285.

5. W. W. Hartup, Adolescents and their friends, in Brett Laursen, ed., *Close Friendships in Adolescence. New Directions for Child*

Development 60 (San Francisco: Jossey-Bass, 1993), p. 9.

6. Berndt, Friendship and friends' influence in adolescence, *Current Directions in Psychological Science* 10 (1992): 156-159; and W. Furman and D. Buhrmester, Children's perceptions of personal relationships in their social networks, *Developmental Psychology* 21 (1985): 1016-1024.

Chapter 2

1. Oden and Asher, Coaching children in social skills for friendship making, *Child Development* 48 (1977): 495-506.

2. Ibid.; and D. Goleman, *Emotional Intelligence*, (New York, Bantam Books, 1995), pp. 250-251.

3. J. C. Masters and W. Furman, Popularity, individual friendship selection, and specific peer interaction among children, *Developmental Psychology* 17 (1981): 344-350.

4. W. Bukowski, B. Hoza, and M. Boivin, Popularity, friendship, and emotional adjustment during friendship and adolescence, in Brett Laursen, ed., *Close Friendships in Adolescence*: *New Directions*

for Child Development (San Francisco: Jossey-Bass, 1993), pp. 23-37.

Chapter 3

1. Putallaz, Maternal behavior and children's sociometric status, *Child Development* 58 (1987): 324-340; and J. Stuller, The unpopular child, *Kiwanis Magazine*, September 1991, pp. 20-23,

2. Coie, Dodge, and Coppotelli, Dimensions and types of social status: a cross-age perspective, pp. 559-561; and W. M. Bukowski and A. F. Newcomb, Stability and determinants of sociometric status and friendship choice: a longitudinal perspective, *Developmental Psychology* 20 (1984): 944.

3. J. Gottman, J. Gonso, and B. Rasmussen, Social interaction, social competence, and friendship in children, *Child Development* 46 (1975): 714; and J. C. Masters and W. Furman, Popularity, individual friendship selection, and specific peer interaction among children, pp. 344-350.

4. E. Hurlock, *Child Development* 6th ed. (New York: M[c]Graw Hill, 1978), p. 272.

5. W. K. Rawlins, *Friendship Matters: Communication, Dialectics, and the Life Course* (New York: Aldine de Gruyter, 1992), pp. 68, 80; and Gentry and Miller, Sociometric indices of children's peer interaction in the school setting, p. 156.

6. W. K. Rawlins, *Friendship Matters: Communication, Dialectics, and the Life Course* (New York: Aldine de Gruyter, 1992), pp. 68, 80.

7. B. Brown, The role of peer groups in adolescents' adjustment to secondary school, in T. J. Berndt and G. W. Ladd, eds., *Peer Relationships in Child Development* (New York: Wiley and Sons, 1989), p. 198.

8. J. Coleman, *The Adolescent Society* (Glencoe, Illinois: Free Press, 1961), pp.35-43.

9. Dunphy, The social structure of urban adolescent peer groups, *Sociometry* 26 (1963): p. 241.

10. N. Cavior and P. Dokecki, Physical attractiveness, perceived attitude similarity, and academic achievement as contributors to interpersonal attraction among adolescents, *Developmental Psychology* 9 (1973): 44-54.

Chapter 4

1. D. C. Dunphy, The social structure of urban adolescent peer groups, p. 235.

2. N. Karweit, Extracurricular activities and friendship selection, in J. L. Epstein and N. Karweit, eds., *Friends in School* (San Diego: Academic Press, 1983), pp. 134-138.

3. B. Brown, The role of peer groups in adolescents' adjustment to secondary school, p. 193.

4. B. Brown, The importance of peer group ("crowd") affiliation in adolescence, *Journal of Adolescence* 9 (1986): 73-96.

5. Hartup, Adolescents and their friends, p. 7; and Epstein and Karweit, Extracurricular activities and friendship selection, p. 132.

6. L. Ellis, Teenagers and Friendship. Louisville Kentucky: *Courier Journal and Louisville Times Co.*, Jan 21, 1990, pp H1+.

7. Dunphy, The social structure of urban adolescent peer groups, p. 238.

8. L. DeStefano, Friendship and Loneliness (Richmond, Virginia, Richmond Times-Dispatch,

The Gallup Organization, March 12, 1990), pp. K1+.

9.   Berndt, Friendship and friends' influence in adolescence, pp.156-159; Hartup, Adolescents and their friends, p. 15; and Aboud, and M. J. Mendelson, Determinants of friendship selection and quality: developmental perspectives, in William. M. Bukowski, Andrew. F. Newcomb, and Willard W. Hartup, eds., *The Company They Keep* (New York: Cambridge University Press, 1996), pp. 102.

10. Bukowski, Hoza, and Boivin, Popularity, friendship, and emotional adjustment during early adolescence, pp. 35-36.

11. Aboud and Mendelson, Determinants of friendship selection and quality: developmental perspectives, p. 102.

Chapter 5

1.   M. Putallaz, Maternal behavior and children's sociometric status, pp. 324-340.

2.   M. R. Radke-Yarrow, C. Zahn-Waxler, and M. Chapman, Children's prosocial dispositions and behavior, in P. H. Mussen, ed., *Handbook of Child*

Psychology Vol. 4, 4th edition (New York: Wiley, 1983), p. 478.

3.   Ibid., pp. 477, 481, 488.

4.   Hartup, Peer relations, 135; Berndt, Friendship and friends' influence in adolescence, p. 156-159; and Newcomb, Bukowski, and Pattee, Children's peer relations: a meta-analytic review of popular, rejected, neglected, controversial, and average sociometric status, pp. 99-128.

5.   Hartup, Adolescents and their friends, pp. 7, 8; T. J. Berndt, J. A. Hawkins, and S. G. Hoyle, Changes in friendship during a school year: effects on children's and adolescents' impressions of friendship and sharing with friends, *Child Development* 57 (1986): 1294; B. W. Laursen, Conflict management among close peers, in B. Laursen, ed., *Close Friendships in Adolescence. New Directions for Child Development* 60 (San Francisco, Jossey-Bass, 1993), p. 51; and B. J. Bigelow and J. J. La Gaipa, The development of friendship values and choice, in H. C. Foot, A. J. Chapman, J. R. Smith, eds., *Friendship and Social Relations in Children* (New York: Wiley, 1980), pp. 36.

6.   Berndt, Hawkins, and Hoyle, Changes in friendship during a school year: effects on

children's and adolescents' impressions of friendship and sharing with friends, pp. 1288-1296.

7. Karweit, Extracurricular activities and friendship, p. 132; Hartup, Adolescents and their friends, p. 7; and Bigelow and La Gaipa, The development of friendship values and choice, p. 21.

8. Bigelow and La Gaipa, The development of friendship values and choice, p. 35; T. J. Berndt, Friendship and friends' influence in adolescence, pp. 156-159; N. Karweit and S. Hansell, Sex differences in adolescent relationships, in J. L. Epstein and N. Karweit, eds., *Friends in School* (San Diego: Academic Press, 1983), p. 121.

9. D. Goleman, *Emotional Intelligence*, (New York, Bantam Books, 1995), pp. 118-122; and S. Nowicki and M. Duke, *Helping the Child Who Doesn't Fit In* (Atlanta: Peachtree Publishers), 1992.

10. J. D. Coie, K. A. Dodge, and H. Coppotelli, Dimensions and types of social status: a cross-age perspective, pp. 559-561; and W. M. Bukowski, and A. F. Newcomb, Stability and determinants of sociometric status and friendship choice: a longitudinal perspective, pp. 941-952.

Chapter 6

1. Hartup, Peer relations, p.135; Hartup, Peer interaction and social organization, p. 393; and A. Newcomb, W. Bukowski, and L. Pattee, Children's peer relations: a meta-analytic review of popular, rejected, neglected, controversial, and average sociometric status, pp. 99-128.

2. Coleman, *The Adolescent Society*, pp. 147-153.

3. Louis P. Nicholson, *Oprah Winfrey: Talking with America*, (USA: Chelsea House Publishers, 1999), p. 8; Sara McIntosh Wooten, *Oprah Winfrey: Talk Show Legend,* (Berkley Heights, NJ: Enslow Publishers, Inc., 1999), p. 36; and Philip Brooks, *Oprah Winfrey: A Voice for the People*, (New York: Franklin Watts, 1999), p. 44.

4. J. Stuller, The unpopular child, pp. 20-23.

5. Gottman, Gonso, and Rasmussen, Social interaction, social competence, and friendship in children, pp. 709-718.

6. W. Sotile and M. Sotile, High-powered couples, *Psycholgy Today* 4 (1996): 50-55.

7. Hartup, Peer interaction and social organization, p. 391; and Newcomb, W. Bukowski, and L.

Pattee, Children's peer relations: a meta-analytic review of popular, rejected, neglected, controversial, and average sociometric status, pp. 99-128.

8. T. J. Berndt, Friendships in childhood and adolescence, in William Damon, ed., *Child Development Today and Tomorrow* (San Francisco: Jossey-Bass, 1989), p. 336.

Chapter 7

1. Bukowski and Newcomb, Stability and determinants of sociometric status and friendship choice: a longitudinal perspective, p. 951; Parker and Asher, Peer relations and later personal adjustment: Are low accepted children at risk? *Psychological Bulletin* 102 (1987): 357-389; and Newcomb, W. Bukowski, and L. Pattee, Children's peer relations: a meta-analytic review of popular, rejected, neglected, controversial, and average sociometric status, pp. 99-128.

Chapter 8

1. Bigelow and La Gaipa, The development of friendship values and choice, p. 37.

2. Laursen, Conflict management among close peers, p. 51; and Bigelow and La Gaipa, The development of friendship values and choice, pp. 35-39.

Chapter 9

1. S. R. Asher, P. D. Renshaw, and S. Hymel, Peer relations and the development of social skills. In S. G. Moore and C. R. Cooper, eds., *The Young child: Review of research* 3 (Washington, DC: National Association for the Education of Young Children, 1982), p.139.

2. Coie, Dodge, and Coppotelli, Dimensions and types of social status: a cross age perspective, pp. 557-570; and Newcomb, Bukowski, and Pattee, Children's peer relations: a meta-analytic review of popular, rejected, neglected, controversial, and average sociometric status, pp. 99-128.

3. K. A. Dodge, D. C. Schlundt, I. Schockenand, and J. D. Deluggach, Social competence and children's socimetric status: the role of peer group entry strategies, *Merrill Palmer Quarterly* 29 (1983): 309-334; Stuller, The unpopular child, pp. 20-23; and S. R. Asher, P. D. Renshaw, and S. Hymel, Peer relations and the development of social skills, p. 139.

4. Coie and K. A. Dodge, Multiple sources of data on social behavior and social status in school: a cross-age comparison, *Child Development* 59 (1988): 815-829; Coie, Dodge, and Coppotelli; Dimensions and types of social status: A cross-age perspective, pp. 557-570; K. A. Dodge, Behavior antecedents of peer social status. *Child Development* 54 (1983): 1386-1399; Bukowski and Newcomb, Stability and determinants of sociometric status and friendship choice: A longitudinal perspective, pp. 941-952; and Newcomb, W. Bukowski, and L. Pattee, Children's peer relations: a meta-analytic review of popular, rejected, neglected, controversial, and average sociometric status, pp. 99-128.

5. Coleman, *The Adolescent Society,* pp. 35-43.

6. Bukowski and Newcomb, Stability and determinants of sociometric status and friendship choice: a longitudinal perspective, p. 944.

7. Laursen, Conflict management among close peers, pp. 49-52.

8. Berndt, Friendship and friends' influence in adolescence, pp. 156-159.

9. T. J. Berndt, Exploring the effects of friendship quality on social development, in W. M.

Bukowski, A. F. Newcomb, and W. W. Hartup, eds., *The Company They Keep* (New York: Cambridge University Press, 1996), p. 360.

10. Berndt, Friendship and friends' influence in adolescence, pp. 156-159.

Chapter 10

1. Berndt, Friendship and friends' influence in adolescence, p.156.

2. Burk, Understanding friendship and social interaction, pp. 282-285.

3. Coie, Dodge, and Coppotelli, Dimensions and types of social status: a cross-age perspective, pp. 557-570; Coie and K. A. Dodge, Multiple sources of data on social behavior and social status in school: a cross-age comparison, pp. 815-829; and Feinberg, M. R., Smith, M., and Schmidt, R. An analysis of expressions used by adolescents of varying economic levels to describe accepted and rejected peers, p. 147.

4. S. Harter, Developmental perspectives on the self system, in P. H. Mussen Ed., *Handbook of Child Psychology* Vol. 4, 4th edition (New York: Wiley, 1983), pp. 348-349.

5. Stuller, The unpopular child, pp. 20-23.

6. Ellis, Teen-agers and Friendship, H1+.

7. Ibid.

8. W. Furman and D. Buhrmester, Children's perceptions of the personal relationships in their social networks, *Developmental Psychology* 21 (1985): 1016-1024.

Chapter 11

1. Oden and Asher, Coaching children in social skills for friendship making, pp. 495-506.

2. W. Furman and D. Buhrmester, Children's perceptions of the personal relationships in their social networks, p. 102.

Chapter 12

1. E. Hatfield and W. Walster, *A New Look at Love* (Lanham: University Press of America, 1978), pp. 34-35.

Meredith Trattler

BIBLIOGRAPHY

Aboud, F. E. and Mendelson, M. J. Determinants of friendship selection and quality: developmental perspectives. In William M. Bukowski, Andrew F. Newcomb, and Willard W. Hartup, eds., *The Company They Keep*. New York: Cambridge University Press, 1996, pp. 87-112.

Asher, S. R. Renshaw, P. D. and Hymel, S. Peer relations and the development of social skills. In S. G. Moore and C. R. Cooper eds., *The Young child: Review of research* 3. Washington, D C: National Association for the Education of Young Children, 1982, p.139.

Berndt, T. J. Exploring the effects of friendship quality on social development. In W. M. Bukowski, A. F. Newcomb, and W. W. Hartup, eds., *The Company They Keep*. New York: Cambridge University Press, 1996, pp. 346-365.

Berndt, T. J. Friendship and friends' influence in adolescence. *Current Directions in Psychological Science* (October, 1992): 156-59.

Berndt, T. J. Friendships in childhood and adolescence. In William Damon, ed., *Child*

Development Today and Tomorrow. San Francisco: Jossey-Bass, 1989, pp. 332-348.

Berndt, T. J., Hawkins, J. A., and Hoyle, S. G. Changes in friendship during a school year: effects on children's and adolescents' impressions of friendship and sharing with friends. *Child Development* 57 (1986): 1284-1297.

Bierman, K. L. Improving the peer relationships of rejected children. In Benjamin B. Lahey and Alan E. Kazdin, eds., *Advances in Clinical Child Psychology*. Vol. 12. New York: Plenum Press, 1989, pp. 53-81.

Bigelow, B. J., and La Gaipa, J. J. The development of friendship, values, and choice. In Hugh C. Foot, Anthony J. Chapman, Jean R. Smith, eds., *Friendship and Social Relations in Children*. New York: Wiley, 1980. Reprint, New Brunswick, N J: Transaction Publishers, 1995, pp. 15-41.

Brooks, P. *Oprah Winfrey: A Voice for the People*. New York: Franklin Watts, 1999, p. 44.

Brown, B. The importance of peer group ("crowd") affiliation in adolescence. *Journal of Adolescence* 9 (1986): 73-96.

Brown, B. The role of peer groups in adolescents' adjustment to secondary school. In T. J. Berndt and G.

W. Ladd, eds., *Peer Relationships in Child Development.* New York: Wiley and Sons, 1989, pp. 183-193.

Bukowski, W. M., and Hoza, B. Popularity and friendship: issues in theory, measurement, and outcome. In T. J. Berndt and G. W. Ladd, eds., *Peer Relationships in Child Development.* New York: Wiley, 1989, pp.15-45.

Bukowski, W. M., Hoza, B., and Boivin, M. Popularity, friendship, and emotional adjustment during early adolescence. In Brett Laursen, ed., *Close Friendships in Adolescence*: *New Directions for Child Development.* San Francisco: Jossey-Bass, 1993, pp. 33-37.

Bukowski, W. M. and Newcomb, A. F. Stability and determinants of sociometric status and friendship choice: a longitudinal perspective. *Developmental Psychology* 20 (1984): 942-952.

Burk, D. I. Understanding friendship and social interaction. *Childhood Education* 72 (1996): 282-285.

Cavior and Dokecki. Physical attractiveness, perceived attitude similarity, and academic achievement as contributors to interpersonal attraction among adolescents. *Developmental Psychology* 9 (1973): 44-54.

Cohen, R., Summerville, M., Poag, C. K., and Henggeler, S. W. A contextual analysis of popularity in the classroom. In Robert Cohen and Alexander W. Siegel, eds., *Context and Development.* Hillsdale, New Jersey: Lawrence Erlbaum Associates, Inc., 1991, pp. 161-181.

Coie, J. D. and Dodge, K. A. Multiple sources of data on social behavior and social status in school: a cross-age comparison. *Child Development* 59 (1988): 815-829.

Coie, J. D. and Dodge, K. A. and Coppotelli, H. Dimensions and types of social status: a cross-age perspective. *Developmental Psychology* 18 (1982): 557-570.

Coleman, J. *The Adolescent Society* (Glencoe, Illinois: Free Press, 1961), pp. 35-43.

DeStefano, L. Friendship and Loneliness. (Richmond, VA: Richmond Times-Dispatch, The Gallop Organization, March 11, 1990), pp. K1+.

Dodge, K. A. Behavior antecedents of peer social status. *Child Development* 54 (1983): 1386-1399.

Dodge, K. A., Schlundt, D. C., Schockenand, I. and Deluggach, J. D. Social competence and children's sociometric status: the role of peer group entry strategies. *Merrill Palmer Quarterly* 29 (1983): 309-334.

Duck, S. W. Personality similarity and friendship choices by adolescents. *European Journal of Social Psychology* 5 (1975): 351-365.

Dunphy, D. C. The social structure of urban adolescent peer groups. *Sociometry* 26 (1963): 230-246.

Elkins, D. Some factors related to the choice status of ninety eighth-grade children in a school society. *Genetic Psychology Monographs* 58 (1958): 207-272.

Ellis, L. Teenagers and Friendship. Louisville, Kentucky: *Courier Journal and Louisville Times Co.*, Jan 21, 1990, pp H1+.

Epstein, J. L. Friendship selection: developmental and environmental influences. In E. C. Mueller and C. R. Cooper, eds., *Process and Outcome in Peer Relationships.* San Diego: Academic Press, 1986, pp. 129-155.

Epstein, J. L. Influence of friends on achievement and affective outcomes. In J. L. Epstein and N. Karweit, eds., *Friends in School.* San Diego: Academic Press, 1983, pp. 177-200.

Epstein, J. The selection of friends: changes across the grades and in different school environments. In T. Berndt and G. Ladd, eds., *Peer Relationships in Child Development*. New York: Wiley, 1989.

Feinberg, M. R., Smith, M., and Schmidt, R. An analysis of expressions used by adolescents of varying economic levels to describe accepted and rejected peers. *Journal of Genetic Psychology* 93 (1958): 133-148.

Furman, W. and Buhrmester, D. Children's perceptions of the personal relationships in their social networks. *Developmental Psychology* 6 (1985): 1016-1024.

Gentry, K. W. and Miller, N. Sociometric indices of children's peer interaction in the school setting. In Hugh C. Foot, Anthony J. Chapman and Jean R. Smith, eds., *Friendship and Social Relations in Children.* New York: Wiley, 1980. Reprint, New Brunswick, New Jersey: Transaction Publishers, 1995, pp. 145-177.

Goleman, D. *Emotional Intelligence.* New York: Bantam Books, 1995.

Gottman, J. M. How children become friends. *Monographs of the Society for Research in Child Development* 48 (1983).

Gottman, J., Gonzo, J., and Rasmussen, B. Social interaction, social competence, and friendship in children. *Child Development* 46 (1975): 709-718.

Gronlund, N. E. and Anderson, L. Personality characteristics of socially accepted, socially neglected, and socially rejected junior high school pupils. *Educational Administration and Supervision* 43 (1957): 329-338.

Hansell, S., and Karweit, N. Curricular placement, friendship networks, and status attainment. In J. L. Epstein and N. Karweit, eds., *Friends in School*. San Diego: Academic Press, 1983, pp.141-161.

Harter, S. Developmental perspectives on the self system. In P. H. Mussen, ed., *Handbook of Child Psychology*. Vol. 4, 4th edition, New York: Wiley, 1983, pp. 267-385.

Hartup, W. W. Adolescents and their friends. In Brett Laursen, ed., *Close Friendships in Adolescence*: *New Directions for Child Development*. San Francisco: Jossey-Bass, 1993, pp. 3-18.

Hartup, W. W. Peer interaction and social organization. In P.H. Mussen, ed., *Carmichael's Manual of Child Psychology*. Vol. 2, 3rd edition, New York: Wiley, 1970, pp.361-456.

Hartup, W. W. Peer relations. In P.H. Mussen, ed., *Carmichael's Manual of Child Psychology.* Vol. 4, 4th edition, New York: Wiley, 1983, pp. 103-196.

Hartup, W. W. Glazer, J. A., and Charlesworth, R. Peer reinforcement and sociometric status. *Child Development* (1967): 1017-1024.

Hatfield, E., and Walster, W. *A New Look at Love.* Lanham: University Press of America, 1978.

Hurlock, E. *Child Development* 6th ed. (New York: McGraw Hill, 1978).

Karweit, N. Extracurricular activities and friendship selection. In J. L. Epstein and N. Karweit, eds., *Friends in School.* San Diego: Academic Press, 1983, pp. 131-140.

Karweit, N., and Hansell, S. Sex differences in adolescent relationships. In J. L. Epstein and N. Karweit eds., *Friends in School.* San Diego: Academic Press, 1983, pp.115-130.

Laursen, B. W. Conflict management among close peers. In Brett Laursen, ed., *Close Friendships in Adolescence*: *New Directions for Child Development.* San Francisco: Jossey-Bass, 1993, pp. 39-53.

Loban, L. A study of social sensitivity (sympathy) among adolescents. *Journal of Educational Psychology* 44 (1953): 102-11.

Masters, J. C., and Furman, W. Popularity, individual friendship selection, and specific peer interaction among children. *Developmental Psychology* 17 (1981): 344-350.

Newcomb, A. F., and Bukowski, W. M. Social impact and social preference as determinants of children's peer group status. *Developmental Psychology* 19 (1983): 856-867.

Newcomb, A., Bukowski, W., and Pattee, L. Children's peer relations: a meta-analytic review of popular, rejected, neglected, controversial, and average sociometric status. *Psychological Bulletin* 113 (1993): 99-128.

Nicholson, Louis P. *Oprah Winfrey: Talking with America*. USA: Chelsea House Publishers, 1999.

Nowicki, S. and Duke, M. *Helping the Child Who Doesn't Fit In.* Atlanta: Peachtree Publishers, 1992.

Oden, S., and Asher, S. R. Coaching children in social skills for friendship making. *Child Development* 48 (1977): 495-506.

Parker, J. G., and Asher, S. R. Peer relations and later personal adjustment: Are low-accepted children at risk? *Psychological Bulletin* 102 (1987) 357-389.

Putallaz, M. Maternal behavior and children's sociometric status. *Child Development* 58 (1987): 324-340.

Radke-Yarrow, M. R., and Zahn-Waxler, C., and Chapman, M. Children's prosocial dispositions and behavior. In P. H. Mussen, ed., *Handbook of Child Psychology*. Vol. 4, 4th edition, New York: Wiley, 1983, pp.469-545.

Rawlins, W. K. *Friendship Matters: Communication, Dialectics, and the Life Course*. New York: Aldine de Gruyter, 1992.

Reese, H. W. Relationship between self-acceptance and sociometric choice. *Journal of Abnormal Psychology* 62 (1961): 472-474.

Roistacher, R. C. A microeconomic model of sociometric choice. *Sociometry* 37 (1974): 219-238.

Scarr, S., Weinberg, R. A., and Levine, A. *Understanding Development*, ed., Jerome Kagan (San Diego: Harcourt Brace Jovanovich,1986).

Sotile, W., and Sotile, M. High-powered couples. *Psychology Today* (July/August, 1996): 50-55.

Stuller, J. The unpopular child. *Kiwanis Magazine*, (September 1991): 20-23.

Wooten, Sarah M. *Oprah Winfrey: Talk Show Legend.* Berkley Heights, NJ: Enslow Publishers, Inc., 1999.

Discover the *Secrets* to:

> ➤ Attain popularity
> ➤ Become outgoing
> ➤ Be self-confident
> ➤ Be charming
> ➤ Hit it off with acquaintances
> ➤ Develop friendships
> ➤ Feel happy
> ➤ Reduce stress and anxiety
> ➤ Solve problems effectively
> ➤ Be academically successful
> ➤ Be a leader

About the Author

Meredith Trattler, a graduate from Emory University, has a Bachelor of Arts in Psychology. She became popular in her teens. Because many people want to be popular and make friends, Meredith reveals an easy, effective plan to accomplish success.